Cuffley
in old picture postcards

by Patricia Klijn

European Library ZALTBOMMEL/THE NETHERLANDS

Cover picture:
A composite card of Cuffley views.
Top right scene is looking along
Northaw Road East towards Northaw. The central view of St. Andrew's shows the hedge and shrubs
that formerly surrounded the little
church.

GB ISBN 90 288 6186 6 / CIP

© 1995 European Library – Zaltbommel/The Netherlands

Introduction

In assembling the material for 'Cuffley in old picture postcards' there were inevitable limitations in the cards available.

You will not find photographs of the early farms in the area, pictures of the old Cabin or much about the railway, the old Schoolroom or the new churches. The work on these subjects was presented in 'Cuffley and Northaw Past' by Gerald Millington and John Higgs, published by Jack Edwards, and in Gerald's earlier booklet 'Cuffley with Northaw'.

Jack Edwards has written and published local histories of Cheshunt, Goffs Oak, Theobalds and Waltham Cross. In numerous articles and talks he has written of Cuffley, its early history and growth.

More recently John Parkes has compiled video recordings of 'Cuffley Memories', combining recollections and pictorial evidence.

Parish Council and Church records are constantly adding to the story of a community rich in groups and organizations. Numerous national charities have networks of enthusiastic supporters, fund-raising at events being documented in their scrapbooks. Conservation and gardening are important in such a well-wooded and rural area.

But the picture postcards are another story. There always were lots of visitors to Cuffley. Cyclists to the countryside, railway trippers, campers in both the Tolmers Scout Camp and the Hertfordshire Schools Camp on Carbone Hill (an international camp in school holidays) and all these visitors sent home postcards bought in the village.

In looking at the cards from even the 1950s and 1960s the changes that have taken place are worth recording. The loss of a telephone box, a tree, or differences in shop ownership are all documented in the world of the postcard. Telegraph poles, vehicles and of course the clothes worn all add to the variety.

Cuffley no longer has G. Biles running a dairy in Station Road or a bubble car parked outside Mayfair, a drapers called Holman or a hardware shop called Churchills. Except on the old postcards. Schools, of course, are at the heart of the community and organizations such as the Scouts, Guides and dramatic societies have always flourished. Detailed records are kept by individual groups such as The Cuffley Players, founded in 1934 from an idea of the Rev. Lionel Sparks, who began performing original works by members of the group, including Geoffrey Orme, a resident of Hanyards Lane. Venue for productions was the old Cabin Hall. The K.T. Company (named after the founder Mrs. Katy Clark-Wiltshire) of Plough Hill produced concerts for the Hertfordshire Fund for the Blind as well as annual pantomimes. An all woman group, the company was formed at the beginning of the Second World War.

Dancing classes such as the Mary Stuart School of Dancing, the Anne Briggs School of Dancing (still catering for the would-be ballerinas of 1995) and Dorothy Taylor regularly put on displays. Victory Parades, pageants and processions all involved the community. A look at old church magazines and ratepayers' books give an indication of the variety and extent of services available over the years. Johnson, the shoemaker at 41 Tolmers Road, Pianoforte teachers in Northaw Road East and The Meadway, builders and watchmakers, could all be found in the documentation of the 1940s and 1950s.

Seekers of other Cuffley writings should turn to the work of Mrs. M. Vivian Hughes (Molly) whose 'London Family between the Wars' tells of her life as a widow with three young sons in a Cuffley cottage at the corner of Oak Lane and Tolmers Road. The building of her new home 'Fronwen' on the East Ridgeway takes place during the book. Characters and neighbours are thinly disguised recognisable Cuffley residents in the 1930s. Cuffley can also boast the originator of the 'Janet and John' school readers. From her home on Plough Hill Mrs. Mackenzie-Wood – or Rona Munroe – compiled the books later criticised in some educational areas for their family bias.

No story of Cuffley is complete without a mention of the SL11 that crashed on Cuffley soil bringing instant fame to the village on the night of 3rd September 1916.

I have included a mixture of 'Zeppelin' postcards, for such it was called on some of them, although later corrected. Hundreds of North London families tell stories such as:

'The Zeppelin came down there, I saw it clear and bright Your Auntie rode out to it from North London on her bike.'

I should like to acknowledge the help and encouragement given to me by Jack Edwards, John and Jeanne Parkes, Alan Gill, Steve Wackett, Gwen Harty, Arnold Jones, Joan McRitchie, Les Clements and Mr. Robert Woods, Headmaster at Cuffley School.

Photographs 1, 30, 50 and 70: Harvey Barton, Bristol; 2, 3, 5, 17, 25-29, 56, 72 and cover picture: Bells Photo Company, Westcliff on Sea, Essex;; 9 and 10: Mrs. Vera Wackett and Stephen Wackett; 12 and 13, Joan McRitchie; 14, 21, 32, 41, 48 and 54: Alan L. Gill; 16: Tim and Gwen Harty; 18, 36, 37 and 39: Rotary Photographic; 22, 23, 42, 43 and 49: John Parkes; 32 and 34: J. Beagles & Co; 33: A.S., 5 Great Titchfield Street, Londen W.; 35: H.B. series 53A Aldersgate Street, London EC.; 37 and 55; Jack Edwards; 38: Press Bureau 1917; 44: Les Clements; 45: Mrs. Hammond; 47 and 73: W.F. Edwards, Graphic Services, Devon; 52 and 64: Hertfordshire Mercury; 58: Basil Edmond and Cuffley School; 59, 60 and 61: Cuffley School; 60 and 63: J.T. Lince, 36 Tolmers Road; 62: Universal Studios, 710b High Road N.12; 71: E. Munnings, Hertford; 75 Arnold Jones and G. Prouse.

We will start our look at the postcards in the main road of the village romantically called Station Road, but stressing the importance of the railway to Cuffley's development. Without it we might still be in 'Cuffa's ley', a grassy field.

Cuffley, October 1995   Patricia Klijn

1 A 1930s photograph of Station Road with G. Biles, the dairy; S. Wackett, newsagent; Holman, draper; Flay and Gambles, electricians; Barclays Bank; Mayfair, sweets and stationers, lending library; Churchills, hardware and W.D. Jones, greengrocer. Theobalds Road, unmade then, Holmes the chemist; A.K.M. Baynton the estate agent, a wet fish shop, Rovers the bakers, a tea lounge and Ripley butchers, and the shops end after the three stepped white roofs. The telephone exchange was not yet built. First telephonist for the village was Olive Pitkin (née Martin) when there were forty subscribers and the exchange was operated from the Cabin Hall in the 1930s. The Standbrook family ran Charrington's Cuffley Hotel. A Bell's Photo Company postcard.

2   A similar viewpoint in the 1950s showing a new lamp erected outside the Birkbeck cleaners, Novelties at no 36, a fine display of dustbins outside Churchills and the new shops built at the top of the parade. Ripleys added a grocers next to their established butcher's shop, Oliphant became Maywyn, wools and drapers; and Chamberlain and Willows became James R. Rogers estate agents. Cuffley Builders was the last shop.

3   A view looking down Station Road with Bayntons acting as agents for the land on which the telephone exchange now stands. Rear views of bungalows in Theobalds Road can be seen on the right of the picture. Cuffley Post Office and Blaxlands grocers (with awnings) are hidden behind the trees on the left-hand side. A public telephone sign is just visible high up on the telegraph pole.

Station Road Cuffley   138322

4   A picture of the original post office building as an estate agents, but interesting, as it includes the police box at the top of the triangle (van parked in front), with the air raid siren on top. The Old Schoolroom, centre of much village activity, is hidden behind trees at the top of the scene. Blaxlands grocers was burnt to the ground and the replacement building, later an off licence, can be seen behind the telephone box.

Station Road, Cuffley.   540.

5　A view down Station Road showing clearly the newly-built shops, including Bradmore Services, electrical goods, between Maywyn and J.W. Rogers estate agents. Note the 'Hovis' sign above Rovers the bakers (Mr.Eddowes) and 'Teas' outside the Tea Lounge. Posted in 1955 this card was 'written aboard the Cuffley flyer'.

616. STATION ROAD. CUFFLEY

6   Station Road again with Charringtons advertisement firmly across the railway bridge over the road. The unmade state of Theobalds Road is clear and as yet no sign of Lambs Close or development on the left-hand side of the road, where the couple walk along by high hedges.

Station Road, Cuffley. 538.

7 A very good view of the sand bin in Station Road and a decorative lamp post. The Lanthorne Café was part of two cottages in Station Road between the Cuffley Hotel and Tolmers Road. The other side of the railway bridge was the Kiosk, a café run by Len Duncombe; Sidney Morris, coal merchant, and the Lulworth Florist, another greengrocer. On the right-hand side a hairdressers Adele has now taken over the former dairy and Perrys have the drapers with striped window blinds.

615. STATION ROAD, CUFFLEY

8   The last in the Station Road sequence but delightful for the bubble car and scooter on what must have been a wet morning, judging by the state of the Theobalds Road puddles. The Cuffley Hotel sign just allows the roof of the stationmaster's house to be seen, later demolished and eventually developed as Laurel Court. There is a double decker 242 at the bus stop under the bridge going towards Goffs Oak. The style of the road signs is also obsolete for the T-junction and the bridge.

Station Road, Cuffley.   544.

9   Mr.Sidney Wackett on the step of his shop at 40 Station Road, with one window given over to a display of Black Cat Craven A cigarettes and wonderful headlines on all the newspaper boards. One even has the day, Wednesday June 28, so the year can be precisely dated on the day a submarine saved fifty or two hundred holidaymakers, depending which paper you read. Three generations of Wacketts have kept the shop going to the present day.

10   Mr. Ralph Wackett, son of Sidney, on the same shop steps with a more modest display of Daily Express and Gold Flake and Players Please. The V.C. initials over the shop were those of Mr. Sidney Wackett's widow Violet. The original shop front was common to the first four shops at the foot of Station Road, a different builder taking over the development at No. 34.

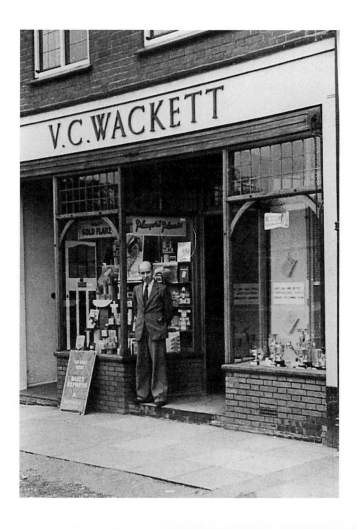

11   Mrs. Olive Fenshom, on the steps of Novelties with her daughter Patricia. This must have been shortly after they took over the business in 1949. The shop was always a glorious mixture of toys, stationery, books and haberdashery, with big names such as Hornby, Kiddycraft and Waddingtons vying for space with all the other products.

12   A 1930s view looking up Plough Hill (or Cuffley Hill Road as it was then called) with fields on the left-hand side before the bungalows were built. The car stands at the junction with what is now King James' Avenue and later the site of Cuffley Free Church.

13 A bungalow at the foot of Plough Hill called Dalkeith. Standing outside are Tony and Joan Upton with Pamela Heyward. Pamela later starred with Freddy Shepherd in roles for the Cuffley Players.

14   Hill Views, says the post-card, but Cuffley Hill Road or Plough Hill are the more usual names. The white flagpole of the Scout Hut is just visible above the hedge on the left-hand side. Note the lack of bungalows at the top of the hill.

HILL VIEWS, CUFFLEY.

15   Cuffley Hill Road
showing the elaborate gates
to some of the bungalows
and development on the left-
hand side. Campbell the
builder displays a board at the
King James' Avenue junction.

Cuffley Hill Road

16 'Rookery Nook', a photograph from 1938 when purchased by the Harty family. It had previously belonged to the Brosnans, who bred 'Scottie' dogs and entered them for shows. At this time the bungalow was approached from Plough Hill. Now it survives as the priest's house, part of the Roman Catholic Church of St. Martin de Porres and it approached via Church Close and King James' Avenue at the Northaw Road East end.

17   Viewed from the triangle on the left of this scene stood the Old Schoolroom and the caretakers house. Mr. and Mrs. Driscoll were resident at the time of this picture about 1950. The site is now occupied by St. Andrew's Church. Another Bells Photo Company card.

Cuffley Hill Road, Cuffley

18   The Plough Inn, Cuffley, much as it was at the time of the SL11 disaster in 1916. The Rideout family were landlords and part of the inn was subsequently used for the inquest into the crash of the airship.

19 A later view of The Plough probably in the 1950s. Numerous changes have been made to the inn over the years; it is still a Mc-Mullens public house and this card depicts the inn before further alterations.

20   The Plough again, not moved round to the East Ridgeway except on the caption. Note the fresh inn sign and side addition and the smart white paint.

The Plough, East Ridgeway.   553.

21	The scene opposite The
Plough showing the houses
clustered round the centre of
what was the old village. The
centre cottages are thought to
be the oldest in Cuffley.

Old Cuffley.

22　Th Nook pictured shortly before demolition in 1994,
to the right of which stood
the pump on the green.

23   The replacement pump pictured in 1994. Originally installed in 1862 the pump supplied the hamlet with its water from a 6,000 gallon tank.

24   A final view down Plough Hill, when brick walls and white lining had totally replaced the rural appearance of the road. Note the lamp post high over the trees on the left.

PLOUGH HILL, CUFFLEY

Photo by Ron Warner

25 Exterior view of St. Andrew's Church on the corner of Plough Hill with the East Ridgeway. Subsequently demolished the little church was much loved, although always intended as a temporary building.

St. Andrew's Church, Cuffley.   No. 3189.

26   The inside of St. Andrew's somewhat resembled the timbers of a ship, but managed to be a welcoming cosy place of worship for the village.

Interior of St. Andrew's Church, Cuffley.

27   Although entitled the Ridgeway this is now known as East Ridgeway and the photograph is taken from the Ridgeway end. Fronwen was built to the right of the picture at this bend. The car is probably that of Mr. Chinchen, the builder, parked outside his house.

The Ridgeway Cuffley.

1383AA

28　A similar view some twenty years later, when trees had hidden the houses, and although the scene is pleasantly rural the photograph was never issued as a postcard. The picture survives in proof form only from the Bells Photo Company, Westcliff-on-Sea No. 1423.

29   The William Leefe Robinson memorial in the East Ridgeway, erected by readers of the 'Daily Express' to commemorate the night of 3rd September, 1916 when Cuffley became the centre of attention as the airship SL11 was brought down near this spot, in fields then behind The Plough inn.

The Ridgeway. Cuffley.

138343

30 A later close-up card of the memorial on a card by Harvey Barton of Bristol. An electric sub-station now stands behind the monument and neat hedges with a gate enclose the area.

CUFFLEY. WILLIAM LEEFE ROBINSON MEMORIAL. 63443

31 The wording on the memorial. Lieutenant W.L. Robinson was subsequently awarded the Victoria Cross for his bravery in shooting down the Schutte-Lanz 11 airship.

ERECTED BY READERS OF
"The Daily Express"
TO THE MEMORY OF
CAPTAIN WILLIAM LEEFE ROBINSON, V.C.
WORCS. REGT AND R.F.C.
WHO ON SEPTEMBER 3, 1916
ABOVE THIS SPOT BROUGHT DOWN
L.21, THE FIRST GERMAN AIRSHIP
DESTROYED ON BRITISH SOIL.

SITE OF THIS MONUMENT WAS PRESENTED TO THE PUB
BY MRS. J.M.E. KIDSTON, OF NYN PARK, NORTHAW

32   William Leefe Robinson
V.C. on a postcard printed by
J. Beagles and Co. from a photograph by the 'Daily Mirror'.
Tragically having survived this
experience he was shot down
over France in 1917 and taken prisoner. But his eventual
death resulted from a bout of
influenza in December 1918.
He was 23.

166.F.   LIEUT. W. L. ROBINSON. V.C.   BEAGLES POSTCARDS.
THE INTREPID AIRMAN WHO, ON 3RD. SEPT. 1916, ATTACKED AN ENEMY
ZEPPELIN (L.21) IN MID-AIR, BRINGING IT DOWN TO THE EARTH IN FLAMES.

33　The 'Robinson' torch is the caption to this artist's impression of the night. This card was published by AS (probably Alfred Stiebel) of 5 Great Titchfield Street, London W. and sanctioned by Censor Press Bureau on 22nd September 1916.

THE "ROBINSON" TOUCH
an impression by an eyewitness - 20 miles away.

Airship brought down in flames at Cuffley, Herts, by
FLIGHT-LIEUT. W. L. ROBINSON, V.C., Sept. 3rd, 1916.
Sanctioned by Censor, Press Bureau, Sept. 22nd, 1916.

34 Typical of the cards published at the height of the popularity of Cuffley after the crash of the airship. Beagles and Co. Ltd. London E.C. published the 'guaranteed real photograph' card passed by the censor.

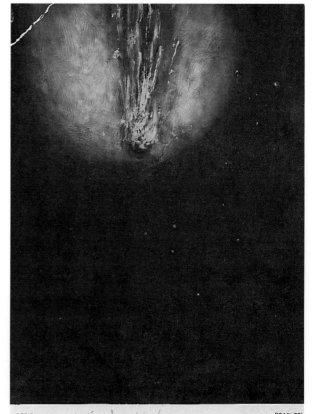

166.G.

BEAGLES'
POSTCARDS

BLAZING AIRSHIP CRASHES TO EARTH.
8,000 FEET FALL.
Sunday, September 3rd., 1916. (PASSED BY CENSOR.)

35 'Zeppelin brought down
in flames' says the caption at
Cuffley, near Enfield. This par-
ticular card was published in
the HB series from 53A Aldersgate Street London E.C.
Note the homes lit up by the
airship and the vivid portrayal
of the airball.

ZEPPELIN BROUGHT DOWN IN FLAMES
AT CUFFLEY, NEAR ENFIELD, AT 2.30 A.M., SUNDAY SEPT 3ʳᵈ 1916.
(DRAWN BY AN EYE-WITNESS).

36   The scene of wreckage after the event. Note the lone soldier on guard at the back of the hedge. Numerous bits of wreckage were either sold to visitors or acquired from the site to adorn the homes of North London. Rotary Photographic card No. 3787A.

3787 A   ZEPPELIN WRECK, CUFFLEY, 3RD SEPT, 1916.   ROTARY PHOTO, E.C.
                       GENERAL VIEW OF WRECKAGE.

37   Another in the same series and a closer view of the wreckage. Royal Flying Corps personnel examine the engine of the Schutte Lanz 11. Rotary Photographic No. 3787C.

3787 C   THE WRECKED ZEPPELIN, CUFFLEY, 3RD SEPT., 1916.   ROTARY PHOTO, E.C.

38   Passed for publication by the press bureau on 10th February 1917 this card was issued by Walker Harrison and Garthwaites Ltd, biscuit manufacturers.

39 A composite card in the Rotary series captioned 'Strafed'.

40 Last in the airship sequence of a later composite card, undated and no publisher, but brought out to confirm that it was not a Zeppelin, and it includes the German airship commander.

At Cuffley Hertfordshire on September 3rd 1916 Schutte Lanz airship S.L.11 commanded by Hauptmann Wilhelm Schramm was shot down in flames by Captain Leefe Robinson flying in a B.E.2c aeroplane.

41   An early postcard of the Ridgeway again showing the rural appeal of 1930s (?) Cuffley. Not a footpath in sight, but telegraph poles and individually-built houses show the development of this road with splendid views across fields to Northaw and Cattlegate.

THE RIDGEWAY, CUFFLEY.

42   The stile, along The Ridgeway, leading to the footpaths crossing the fields to Northaw on one of the area's popular walks. Pictured on the stile is Pamela Yeomans on a visit to her aunt in Kingsmead from her home in Southgate.

43   The building of Ekna Cottage further along The Ridgeway on the left-hand side towards the Carbone Hill junction. Mr. Alfred Neill is photographed with his dog Waggy at the rear of the bungalow during the early 1930s.

44   Another important route in Cuffley is Tolmers Road. For many years unmade it has always had a variety of individual houses and bungalows. Here is the stationmaster's house, seen boarded up and shortly before demolition in December 1981. Laurel Court now occupies the site.

45   Cuffley Station on Easter
Monday 1971, with the old
type signal and the signal box
just visible by the train on the
way to Hertford North. Note
the Cuffley sign in the waiting room window just be-
hind the wooden seat and the
buckets just outside the por-
ter's room. Oak Lane cottages
are just noticeable above the
roof of the waiting rooms.

46   Tolmers Road under-
going some repairs with the
words 'Private Road' promi-
nently displayed to the left
centre of the picture.

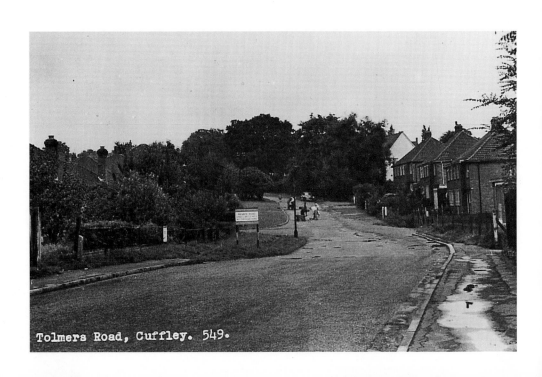

Tolmers Road, Cuffley. 549.

47   A similar view, the notice now reading: 'Please drive slowly. No footpaths.' Hedges have gone and the motor car is taking over. A photograph by W.F. Edwards of Graphic Services, Devon, who regularly visited the village to take his pictures for viewcards.

224/9

Tolmers Road, Cuffley

48   A little further up a view of Tolmers Road at the junction with Acorn Lane on the left. The house on the left was for many years the home of Mr. Johnson, the shoemaker, and was later occupied by the Gibb family. Still no pathways.

Tolmer Road, Cuffley

49   Cottages on Tolmers Road at the corner of Oak Lane, photographed shortly before considerable alterations to the cottage on the right of the picture. This was for many years home of the Cuffley writer Mrs. M.V. Hughes, her book 'A London Family between the Wars' telling of Cuffley and the locality.

50   The far end of Tolmers Road at the junction with Homewood Avenue. The road leads straight on to footpaths through the Home Wood to Carbone Hill. Trees on the right are at the entrance to perhaps one of Cuffley's most famous spots: the Tolmers Scout Camp. Hundreds of boys have enjoyed outdoor life in the extensive grounds and to many 'Cuffley' still means idyllic days spent in Tolmers Camp.

51   Kingsmead at the top of Plough Hill, not quite turned into a postcard, but evocative of Cuffley's development as a residential area.

52 Kingsmead again, The Plough is at the back of this picture with the Scouts under starters orders from Skipper Lionel Gill for the regular cart race.

53 Cuffley and Northaw Youth Centre at the foot of Cuffley Hill, which has been another centre for the community for many years. As well as providing a much needed facility as a Youth Centre, the building has been home to fetes, fashion shows, amateur dramatics, dog shows and charitable events.

CUFFLEY & NORTHAW YOUTH CENTRE

54   The road as it used to be just past the Youth Centre. Brook Farm is on the left with a car and pedestrians at the farm entrance. Note that there is no path at all on the hill up to Goffs Oak.

CUFFLEY HILL.

55　A similar view taken a
little nearer the bridge over
the Cuffley Brook. Note the
child walking towards the ca-
mera on the left. This card
was published by Gordon
Smith of 15 Stroud Green
Road, London N.

1448　Road to Goffs Oak, Cuffley.

56   A view down Cuffley Hill towards the scenes in the previous pictures. Good for the request bus stops and the car parked quite comfortably on what is now a busy main route.

Cuffley Hill.   No. 1424

57   St. James' School, Goffs
Oak. Another photographer's
sample card that did not quite
get to be a postcard, but it
gives a fine historical record
of the former village school at
Goffs Oak.

58   Interior view of Cuffley School at the end of Theobalds Road and South Drive. A nostalgic picture, in 1950, taken by Mr. Basil Edmond, a former teacher at the school.

59 Group Cuffley School photograph taken in 1946. The names of the children where known are as follows, left to right, top row: Terry Hinson, Terry Hockley, (?), Janet Hilliard, Miss Dorothy Ogborn (teacher), Barbara Purkington, Janet Linsell, David Seager, Robin Burley and John Finnemore. Second row: Charlie Brace, Derek Gearing, Iris Rolls, Pat Fenshom, Hazel James, (?) Howard Gates and Roger Wilkes. Third row: Edward Baker, (?) June Amis, (?) Sinclair Scott, Michael Ayre, Judy Hiscock, (?), Norma Ponder and (?). Fourth row: David Jones, Ian Wright, Maureen Chapman, Pamela Cowell, Jean Roser, (?), Susan Thurgood, Dorothy Warner and two unknown.

60   Many of the same children taken in 1948 with class teacher Mr. Phillips. Names where known are: David Jones, Robert Hardwick, Terry Hinson, Robin Burley, Derek Gearing, David Seager and John Duncombe. Second row, left to right: Janet Hilliard, Judy Hiscock, Pat Richardson, Ivy Richardson, Margaret Blackford, Jennifer Morris and Maisie Thrussell. Front row: Pamela Cowell, Avril Sare, Janet Linsell, Ann Norris, Maureen Chapman, Iris Rolls, Susan Thurgood, Annette Buckler and Pat Fenshom.

61 A Cuffley school photograph taken in 1946 of Mrs. Allingham's class of leavers.

62 The final term of the Guildhouse School on Carbone Hill. The group comprises the boarders and resident staff in the summer of 1956. Seated, left to right, are: Pat Fenshom, Matron, Miss Mary Smith and Miss Harriet Smith, principals of the school, and Peggy Eagle. The school occupied two houses, one of which later became the home of Dr. Reynolds.

63   A group photograph of Guides and Rangers taken inside the Old Schoolroom, since demolished to make way for St.Andrew's Church. Left to right, top row: Mavis Bennett, Pat Hussey, Hetty Young, Audrey Whittle, Mary Gill, Pat Beale, Angela Hayes, seated Joan Edwards(?), (?), Nancy Marriner, Guide Captain and Margaret Willmott. Second row: Ruth Ogborn, (?), Christine Shackcloth, June Amis, Pamela Wright, (?), Susan Thurgood, Janet Hilliard, Pat Fenshom. Front row: Margaret Giles, Judy Barber, Anthea Beverley, Elizabeth Hall, Dawn Candy, (?) and Christine Ford.

64　Another group in the Old Schoolroom (1950s), including Brownies Marilla Kelly, Gillian Gathercole, Rhona and Wendy Gentle, Vivienne Allingham, Lynne Harty, Susan McEvoy and Paula Lince. Brown Owl Mrs. Blackford with helper and her daughter Pat and Pat Fenshom.

65   The delightful old cottage formerly at the junction of Carbone Hill with the Ridgeway. Note the finger post on the left of the scene with the directions to Newgate Street and Hertford and the bicycle wheel. The cottage was thought by some to have once been a toll house. The postcard was used to announce the safe arrival of children at the Camp.

66 'Cuffley Woods', states the caption, although it has to be admitted it could be anywhere. What would be marvellous would be to identify the two young ladies in the photo carrying what looks like armfuls of bluebells. The postcard is unused and no printer's marks or dates can help.

CUFFLEY WOODS.

67   Up at Newgate Street the lodge at the entrance to Tolmers Hospital is still occupied, after extensive refurbishments to the buildings and the original hospital.

68   Tolmers Park Hospital as
it was before conversion. It
was for many years a hospital
for the elderly.

69   Newgate Street Village. Teas are obtainable at the cottage on the right and a notice on the left proclaims; 'Local Postcards sold here.'

NEWGATE STREET.

70   Ponsbourne, St. Mary's
Church in Newgate Street Village.

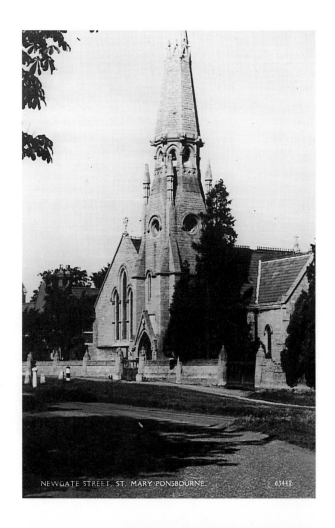

NEWGATE STREET, ST. MARY PONSBOURNE.   63112

71   Ponsbourne House in the Ponsbourne Park at Newgate Street. E. Munnings of Hertford produced this postcard and it was posted from there in 1906. Hertford has always claimed Newgate Street and its inclusion in this little book puts on record another building that has undergone many changes of ownership and usage.

Ponsbourne House, near Hertford   E. Munnings, Hertford

72   Leading out of Cuffley in the other direction along Northaw Road East is this photo of about the 1950s, without footpaths on the right of the picture and many original gates to the bunga-lows.

Northaw Road, Cuffley.

138340

73   This postcard of the view across the fields to The Ridgeway on the horizon is taken from the Northaw Road. Typical of the undulating countryside, the scene shows the wooded area of The Dell in the distance and hedged farmland.

74   The Parish Church of St. Thomas of Canterbury, Northaw, pictured from the Potters Bar direction and showing the war memorial on the village green.

NORTHAW PARISH CHURCH

75　The picture of Cyril G. Prouse at Northaw pump was taken by his father, George Bertram Prouse, about 1924. The original of this photograph was taken from a magic lantern slide. Cyril Prouse now lives at Leighton Buzzard.

76   Left: another composite 'Cuffley and District' card, including churches at Northaw and Newgate Street. The thatched cottage at Flamstead End was one of the lodge cottages to Cheshunt Park.

Right: reproductions of old postcards in a composite card showing Lower Hanyards Farm top left, the Old Schoolroom and the caretaker's house bottom left, and The Plough Inn with Hill Farm entrance gate in the bottom right scene.